AF380904

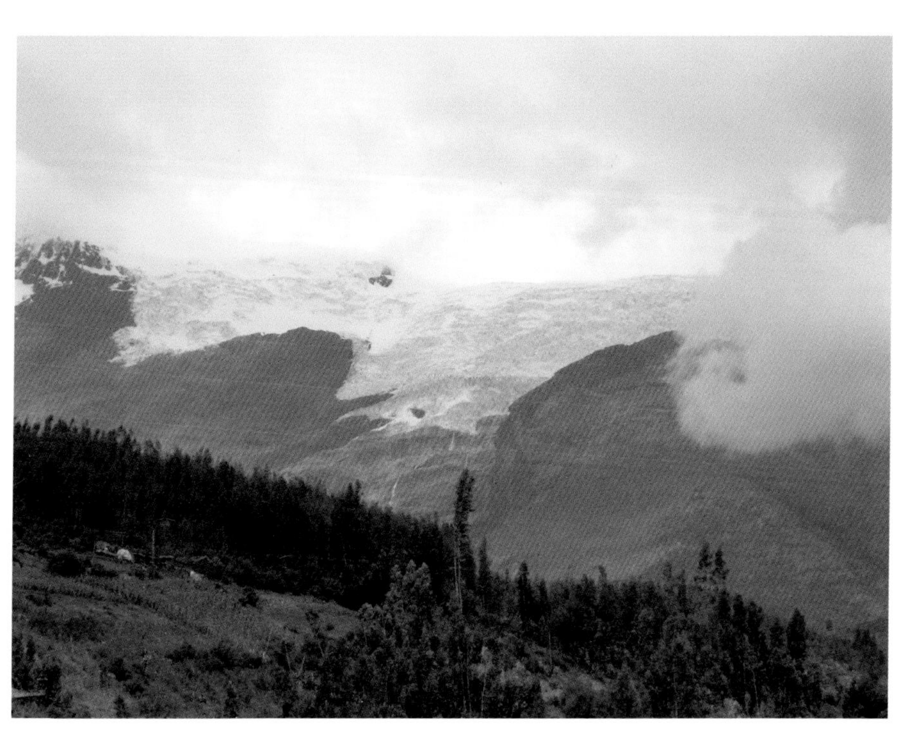

ARCHIVE

Danielle Mericle

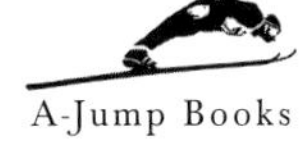

A-Jump Books

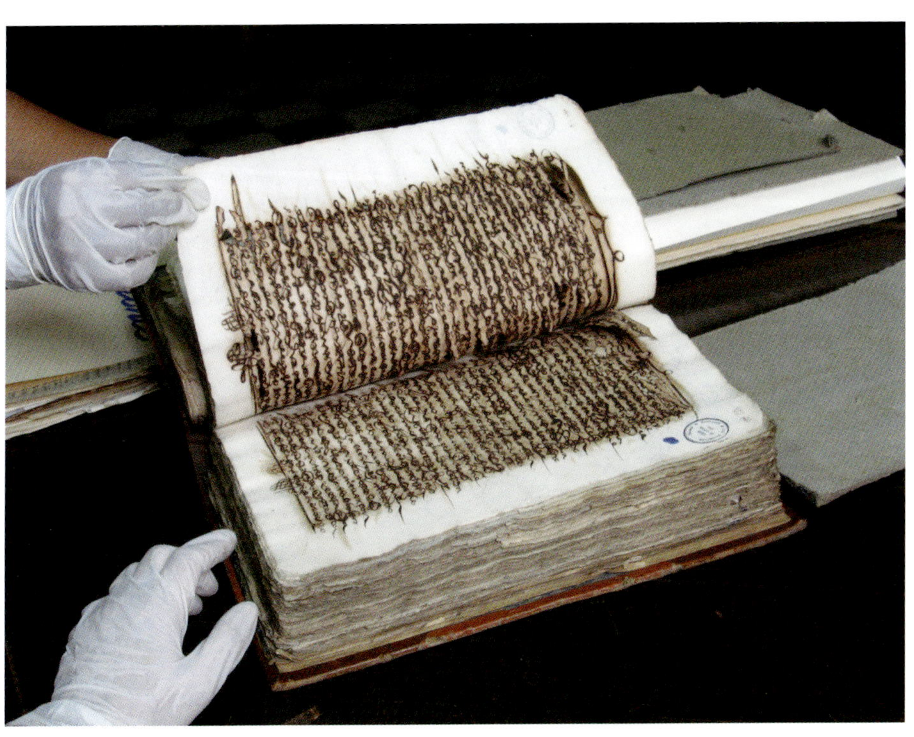

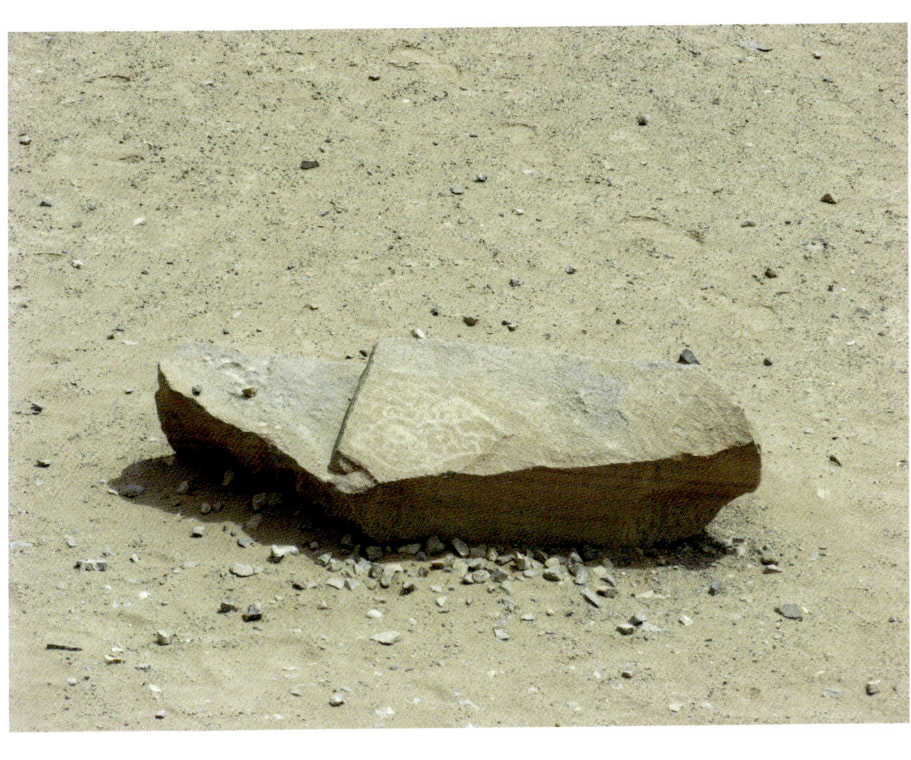

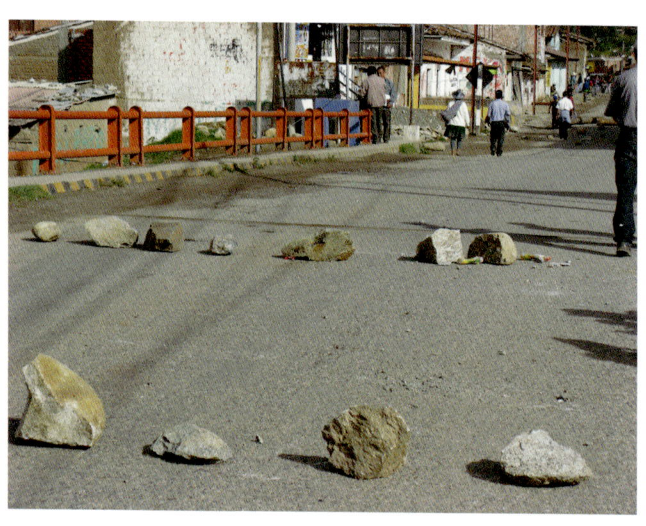

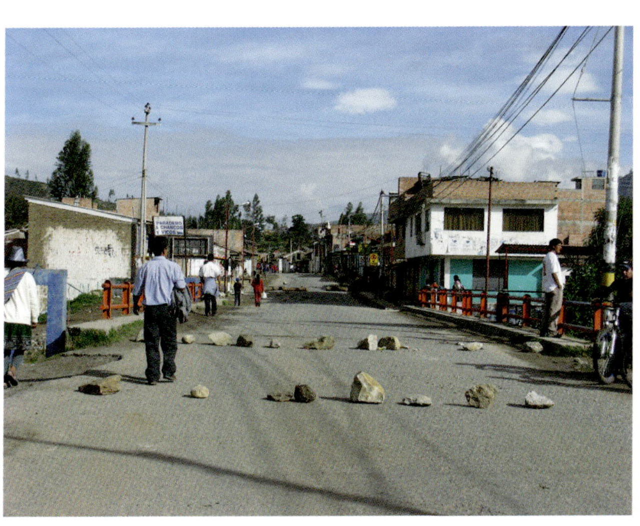

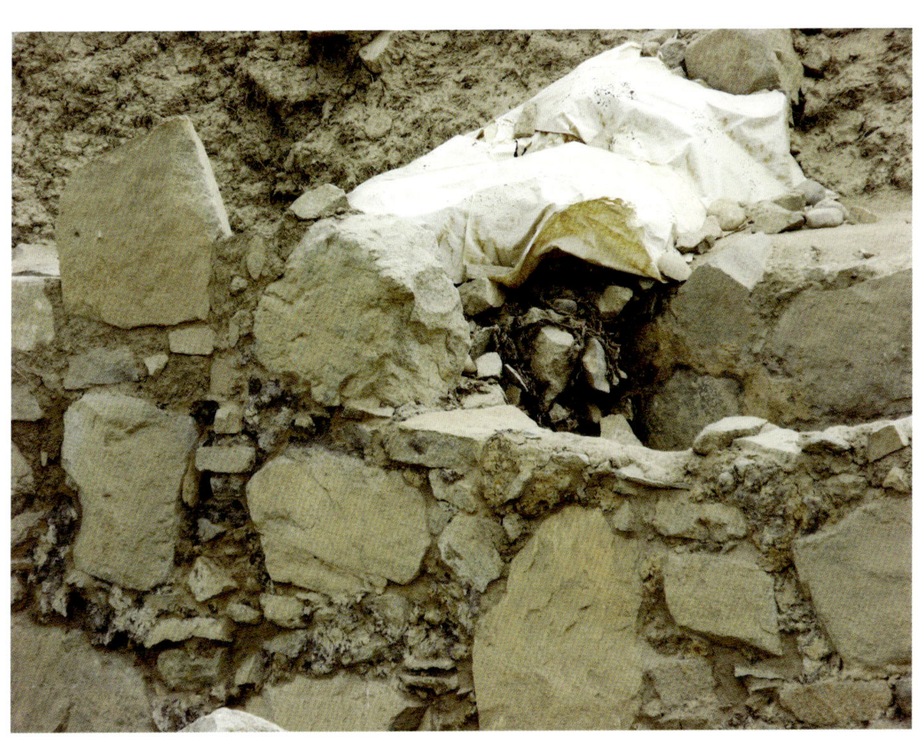

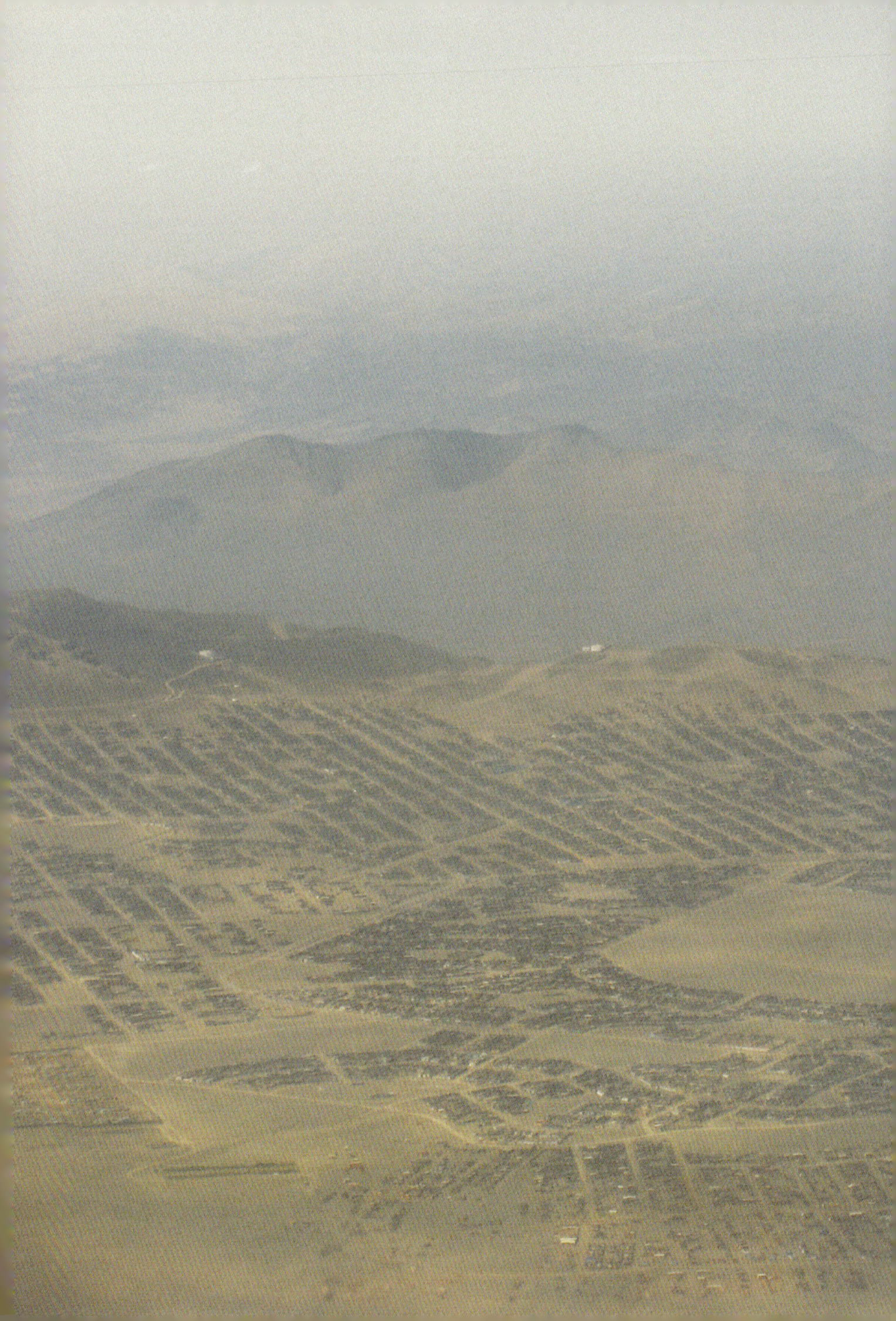

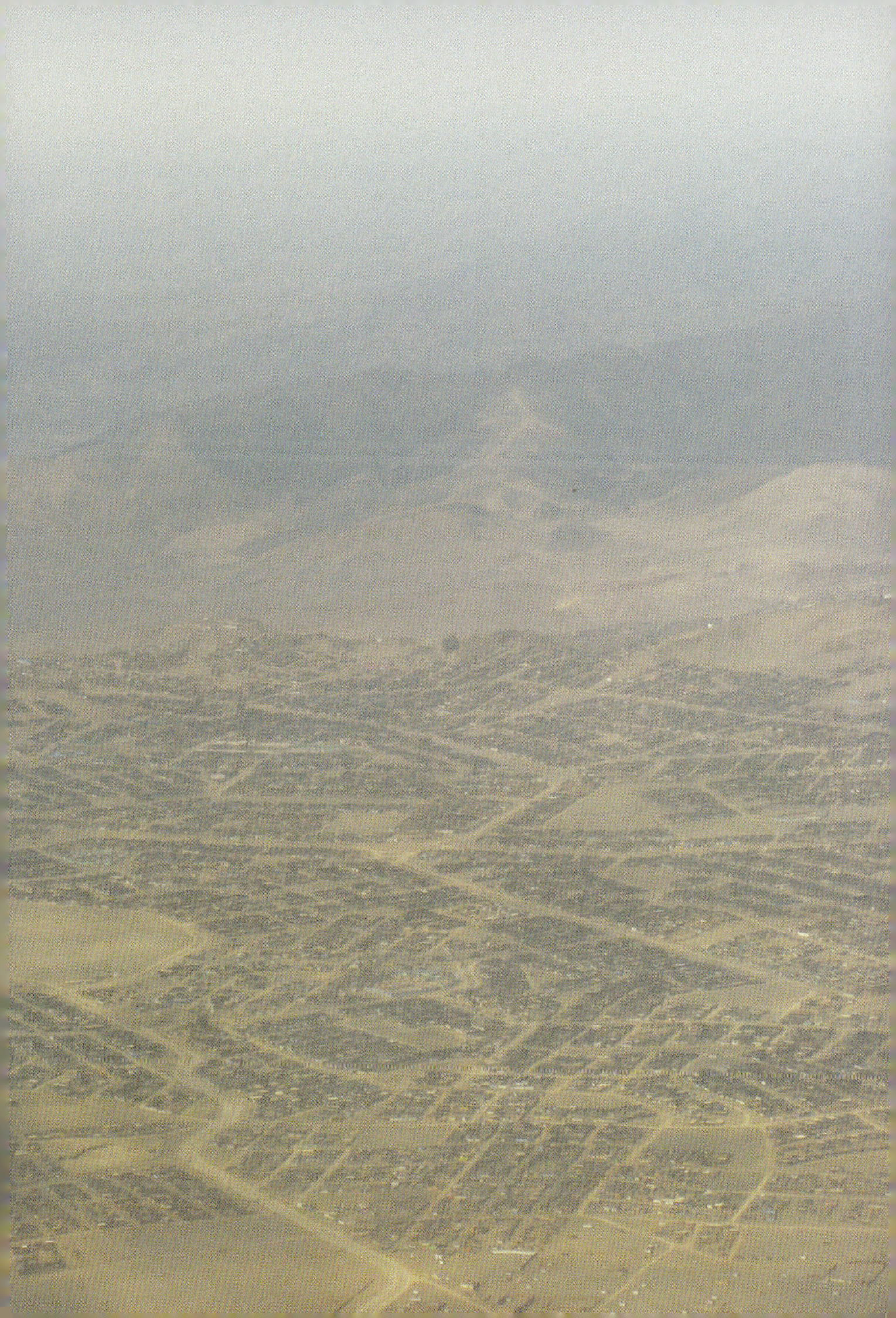

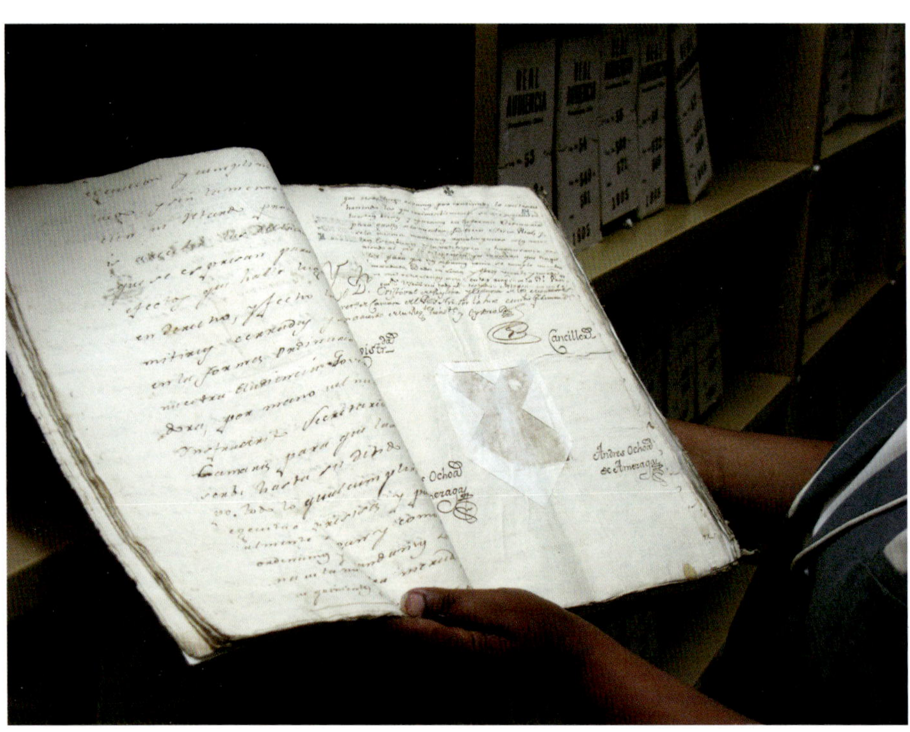

Cancilla
Andres Ochoa de Amezaga

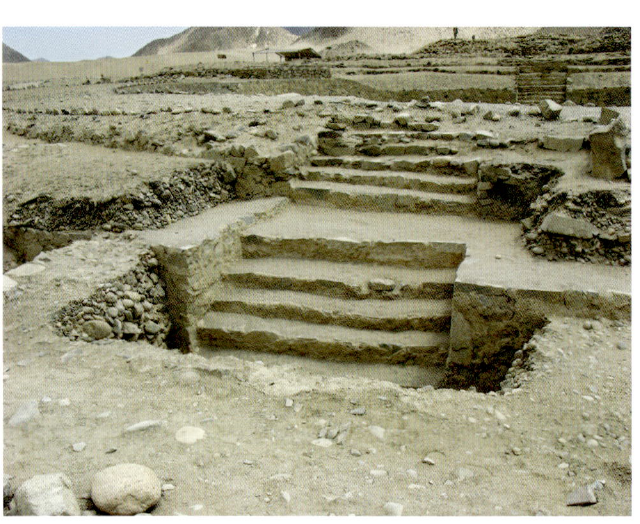

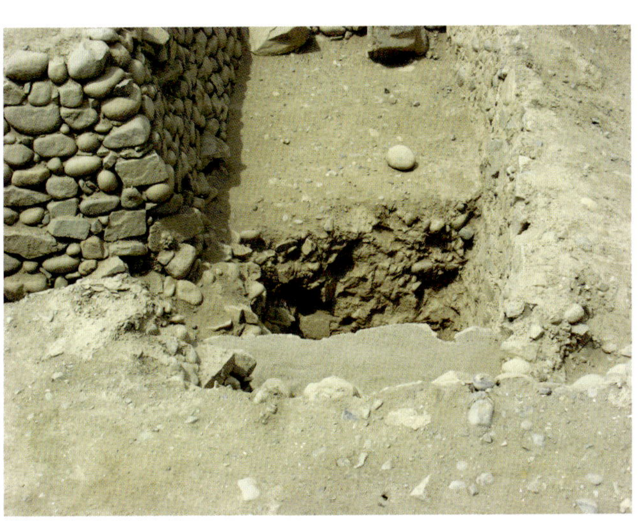

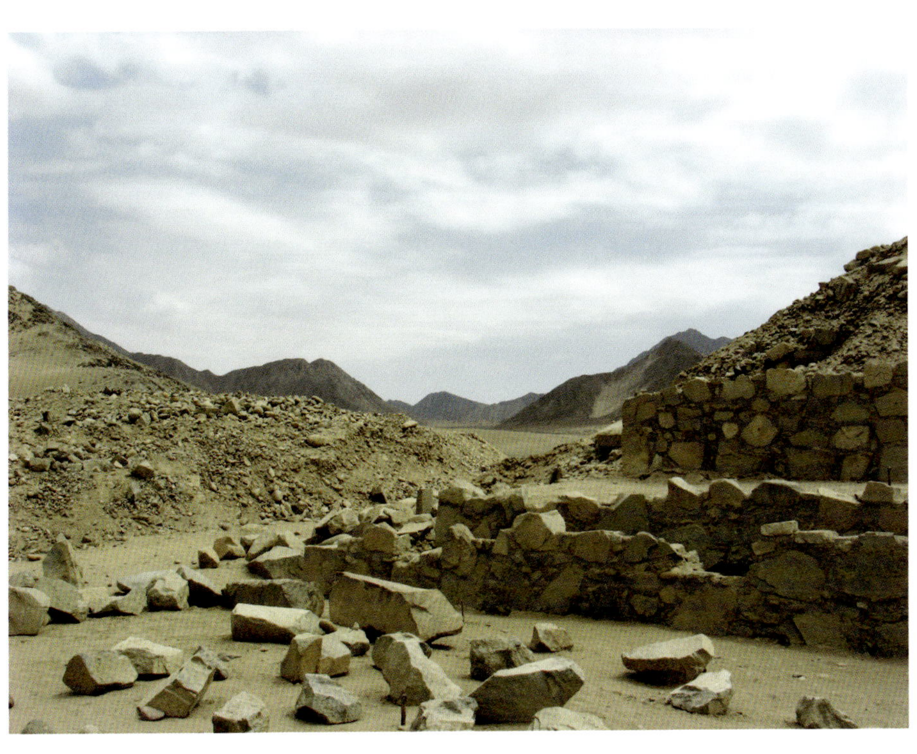

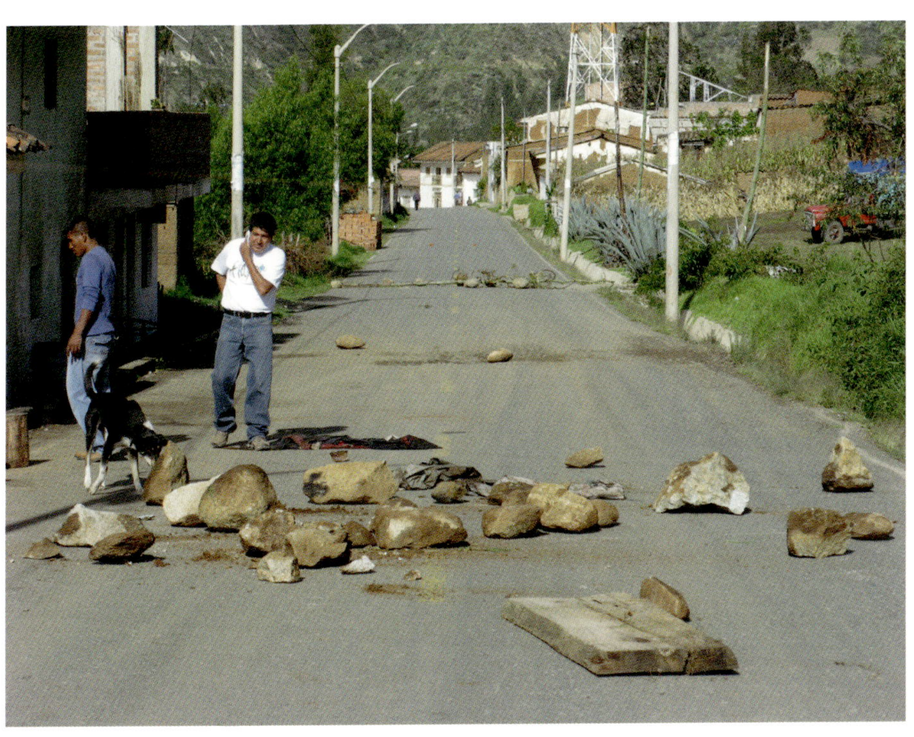

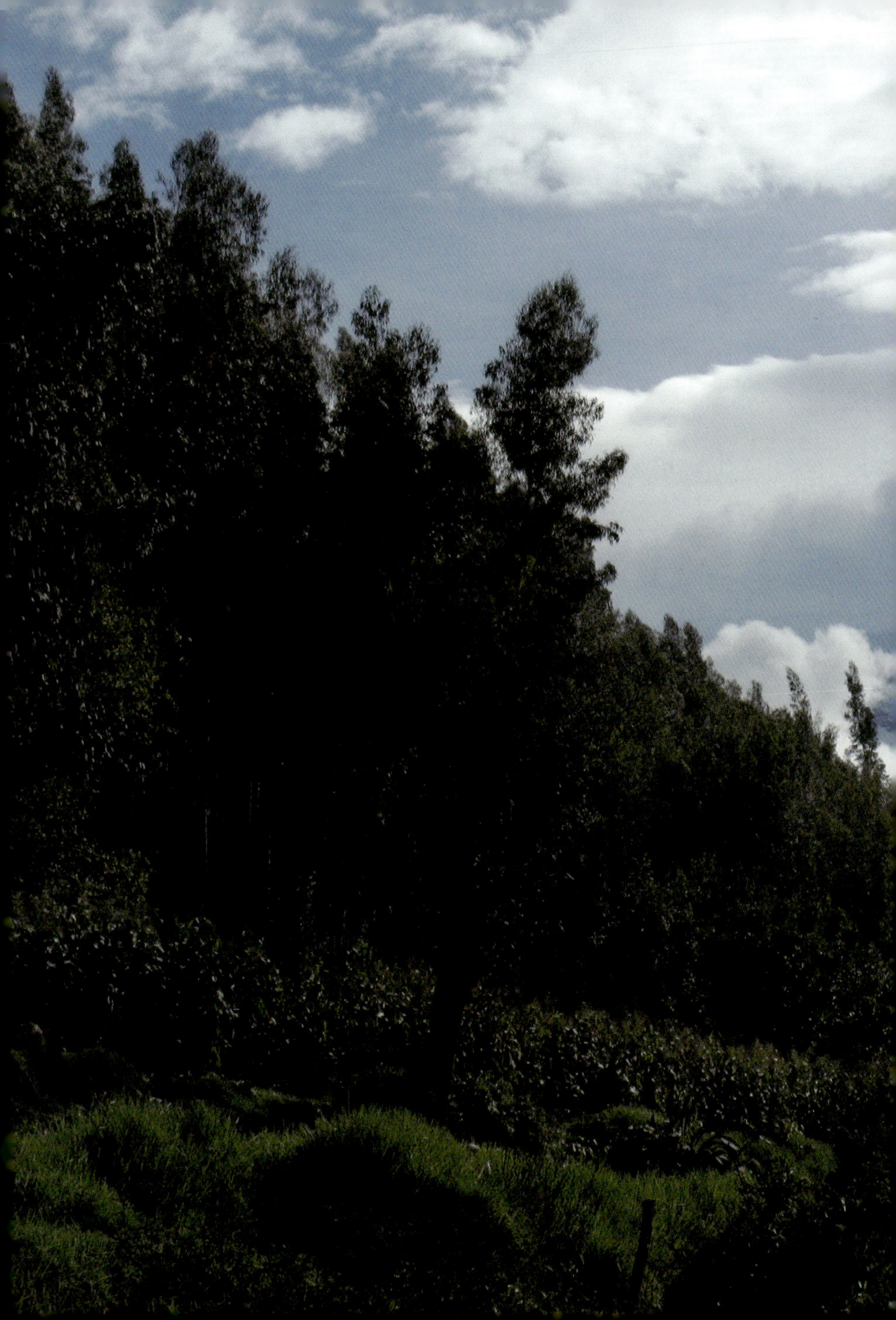

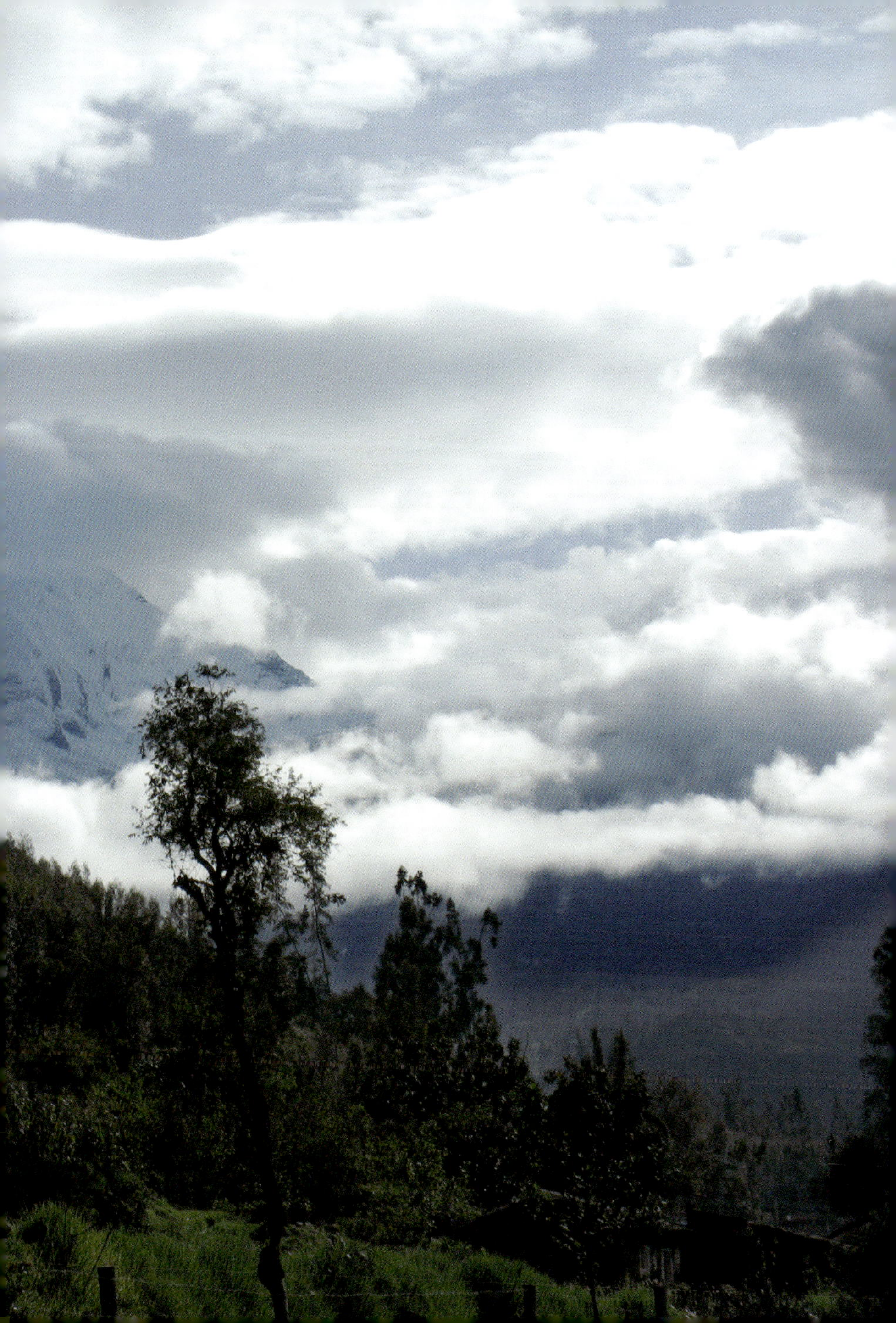

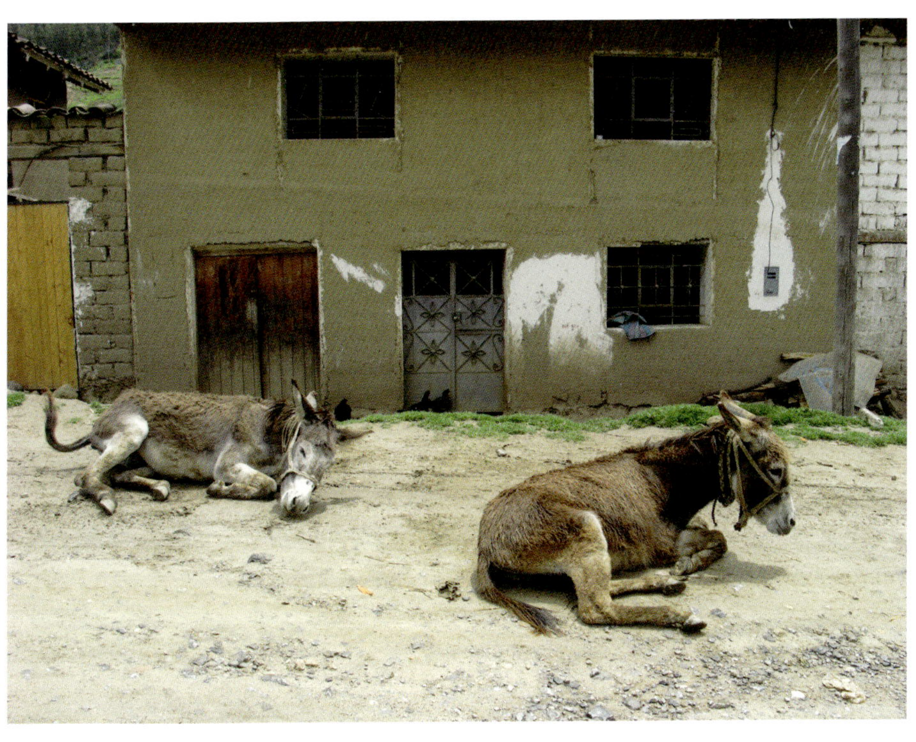

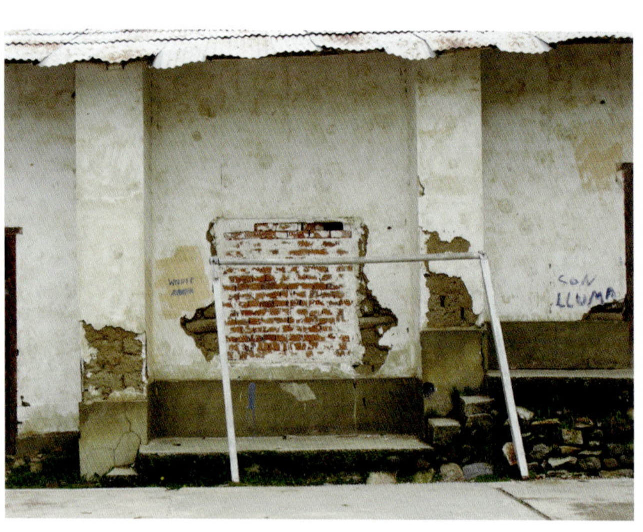
CON
LLUMA

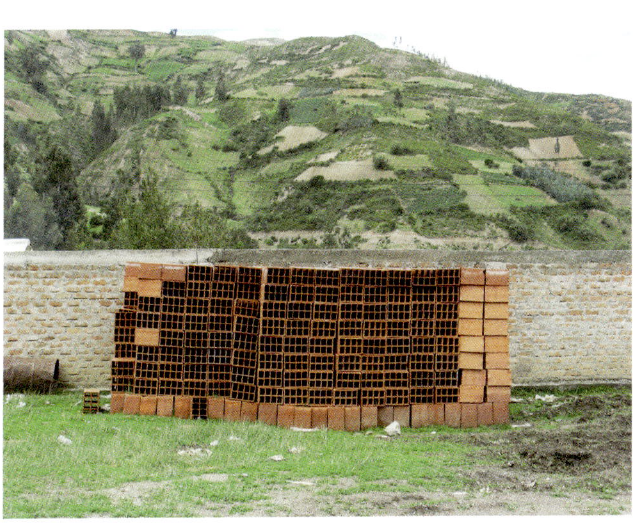

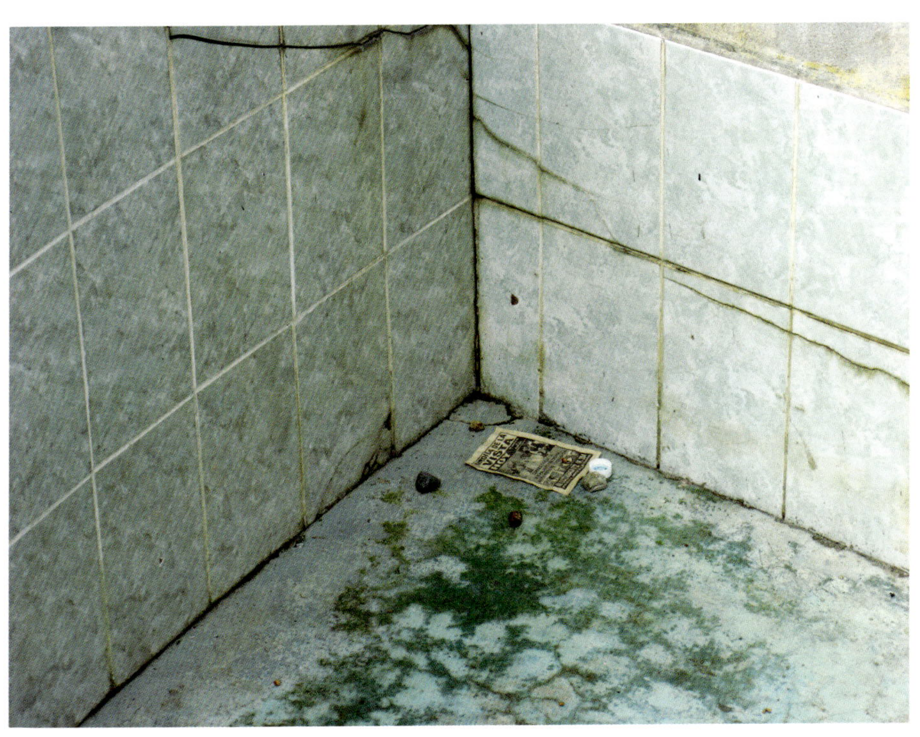

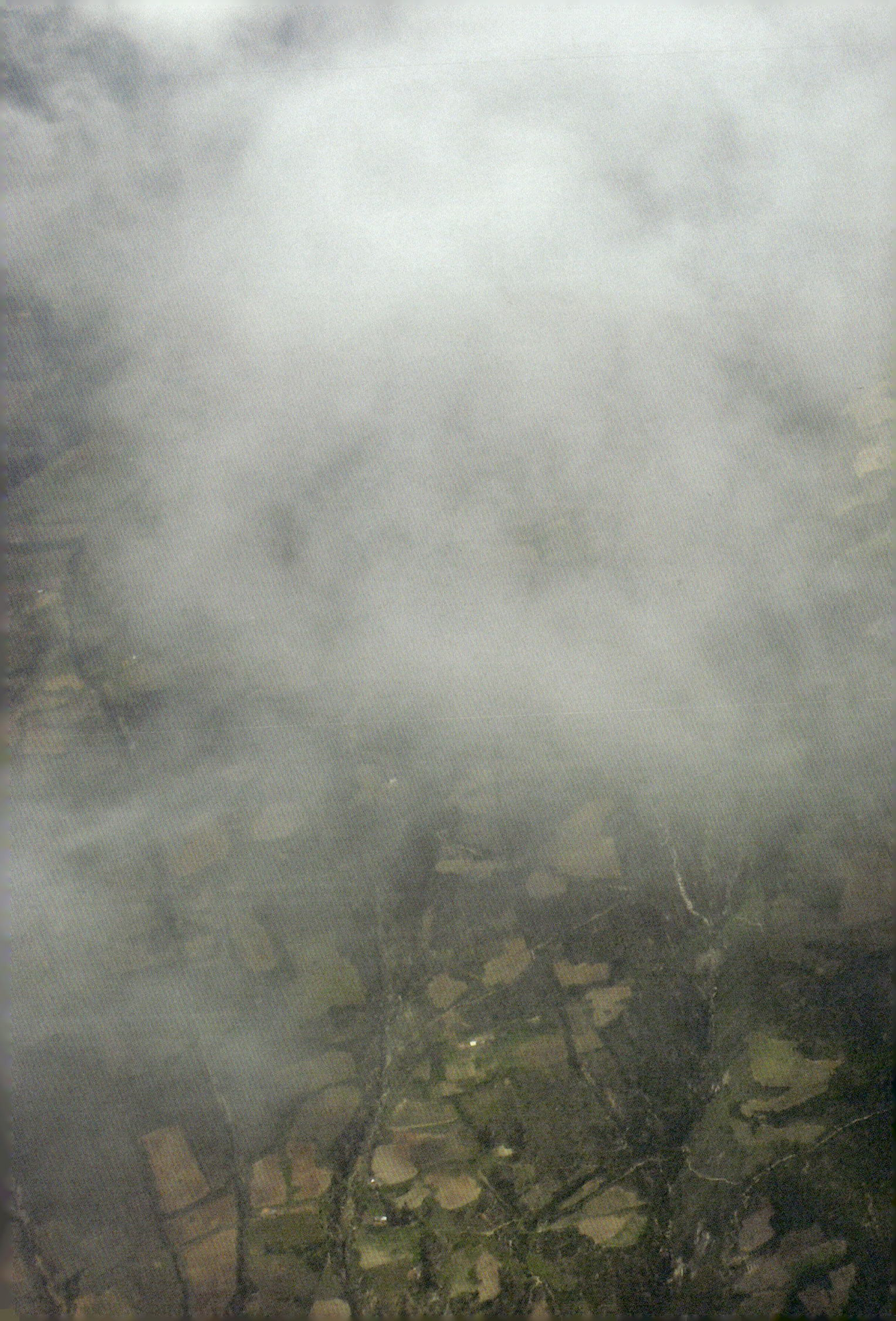

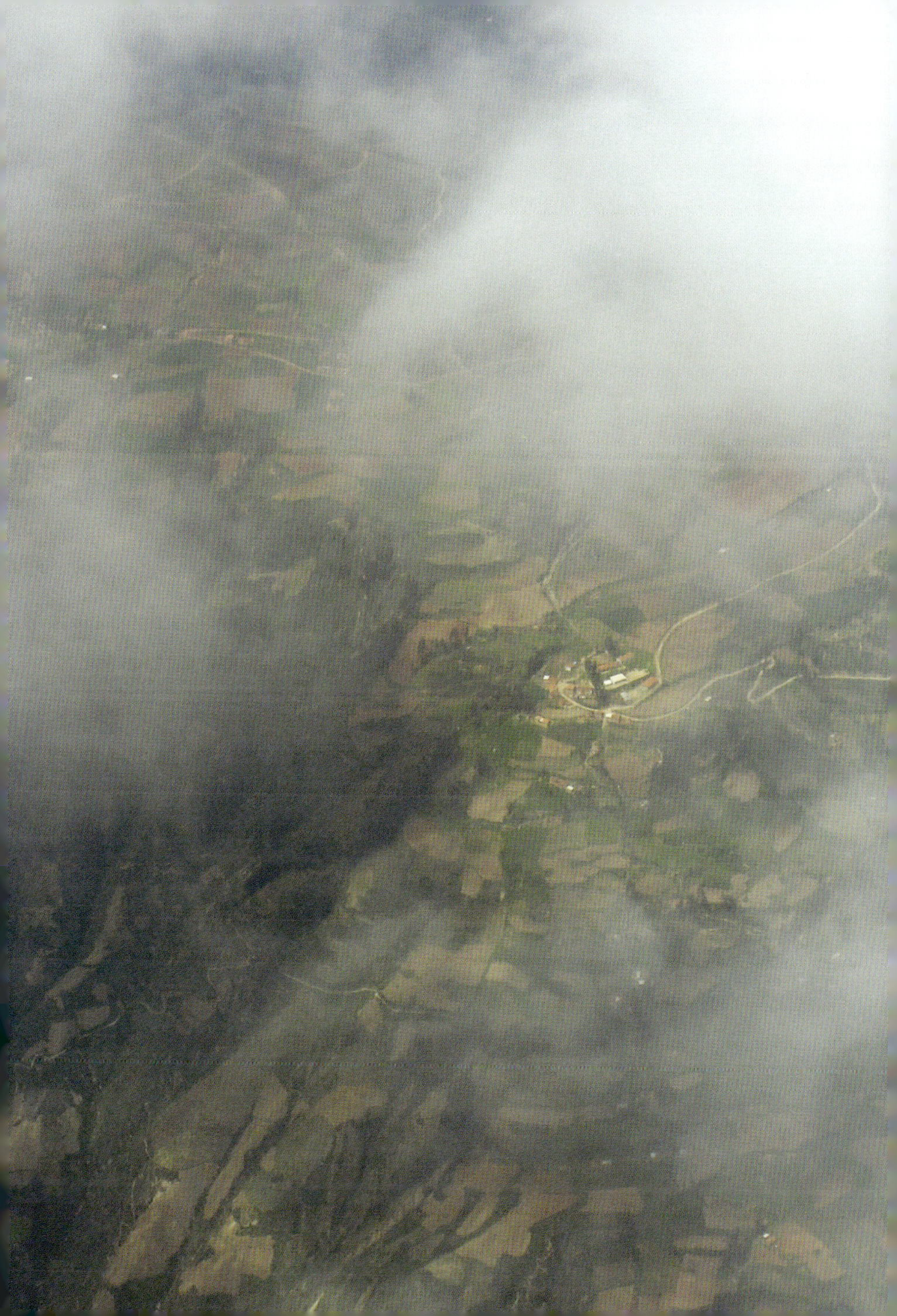

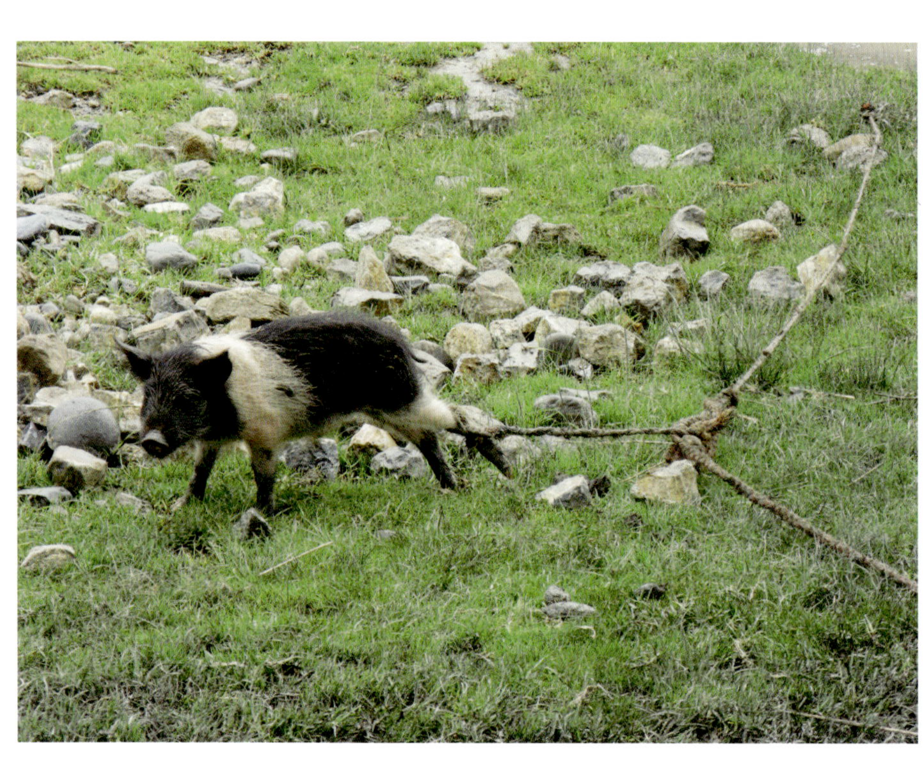

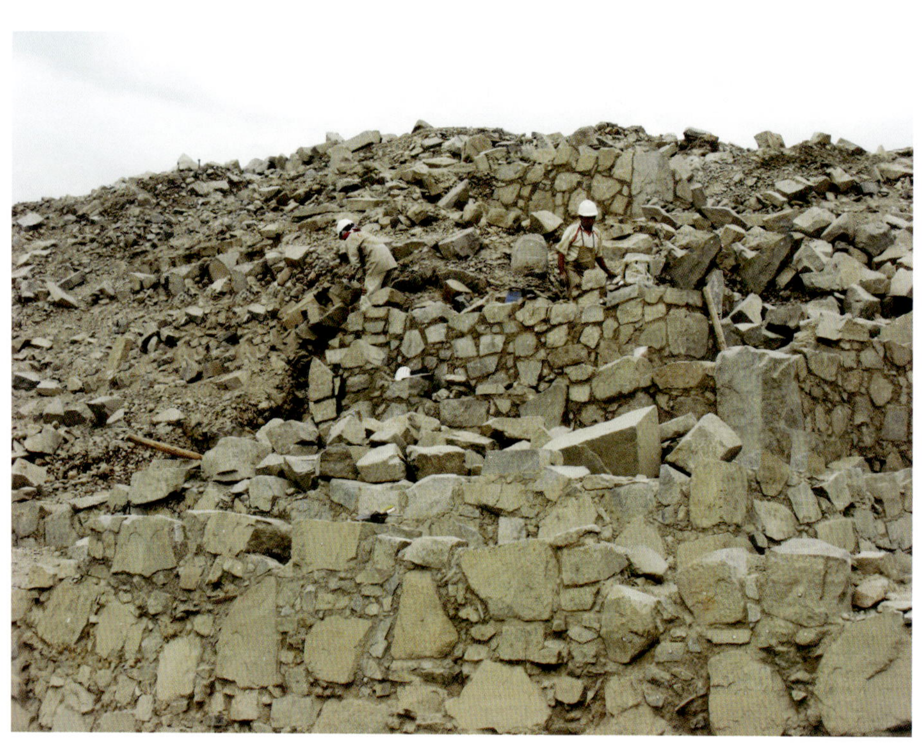

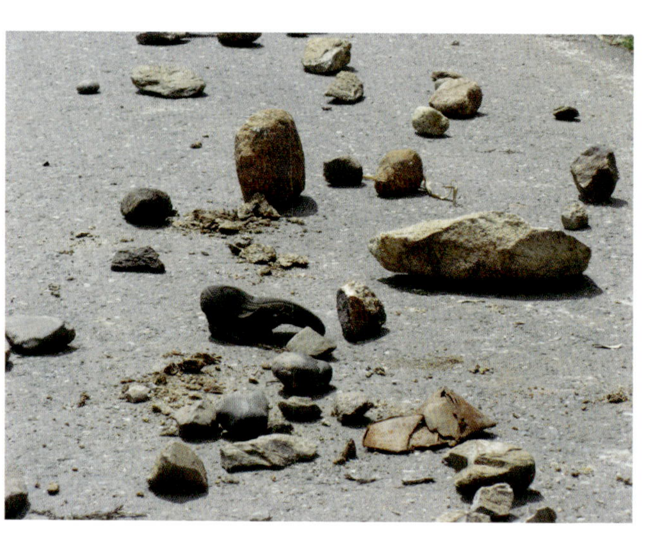

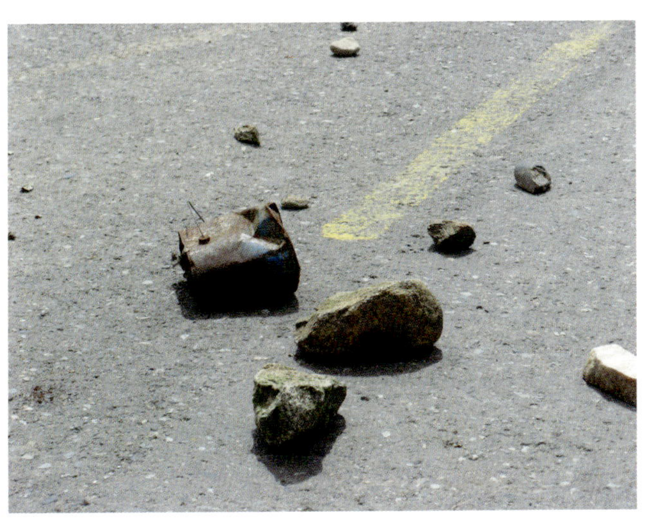

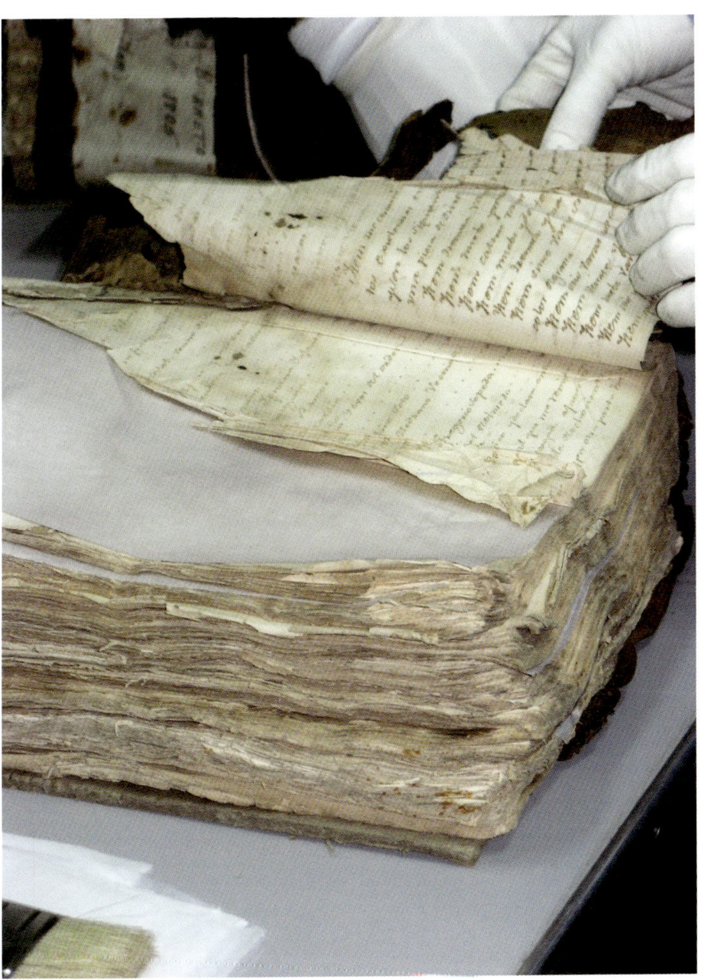

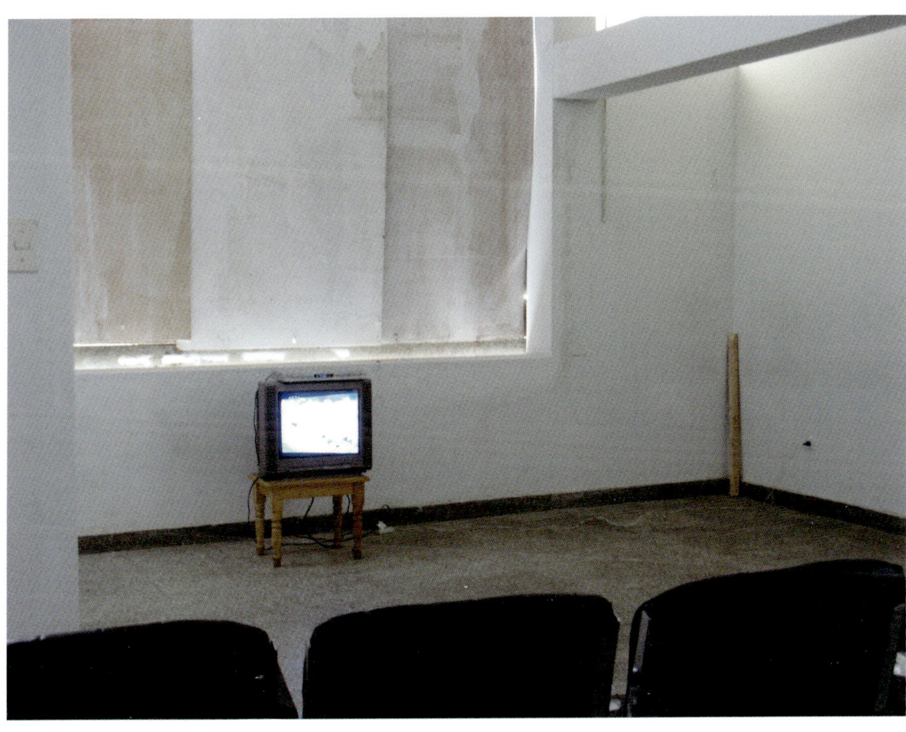

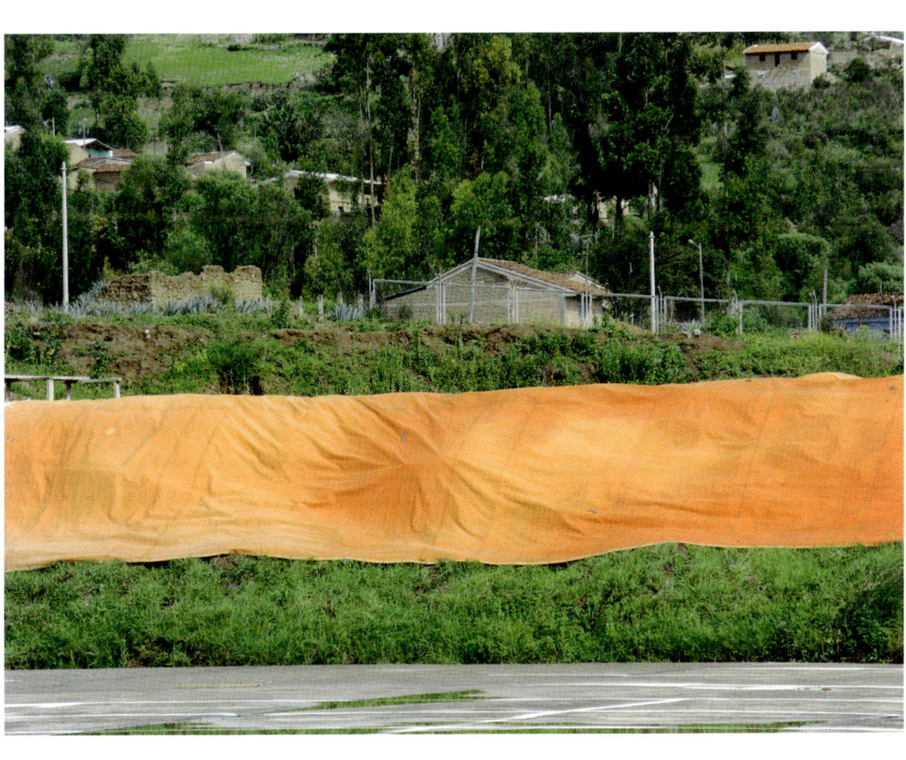

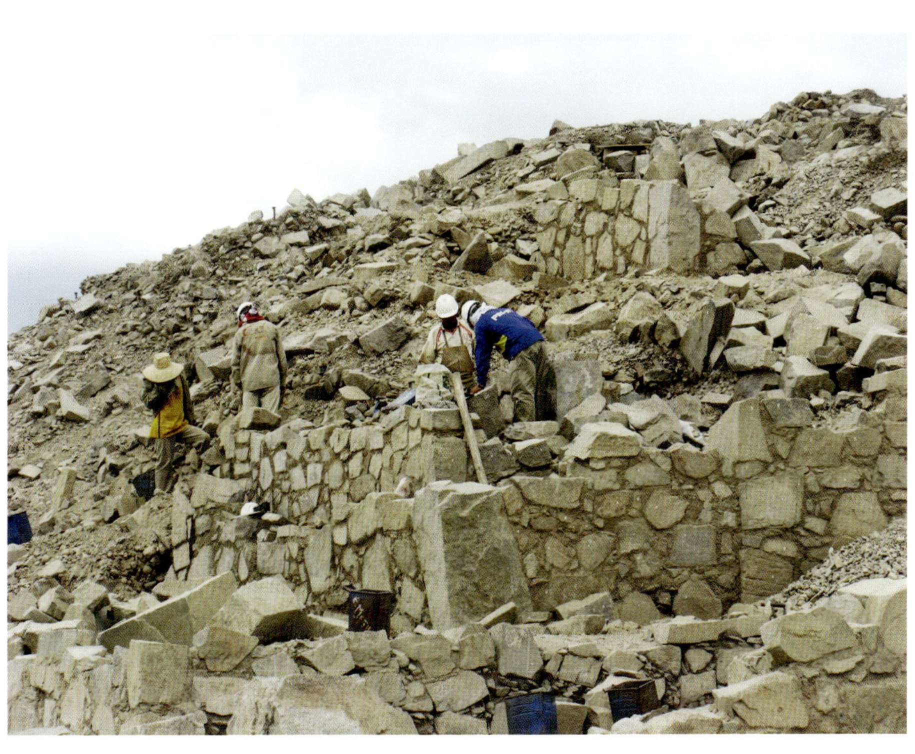

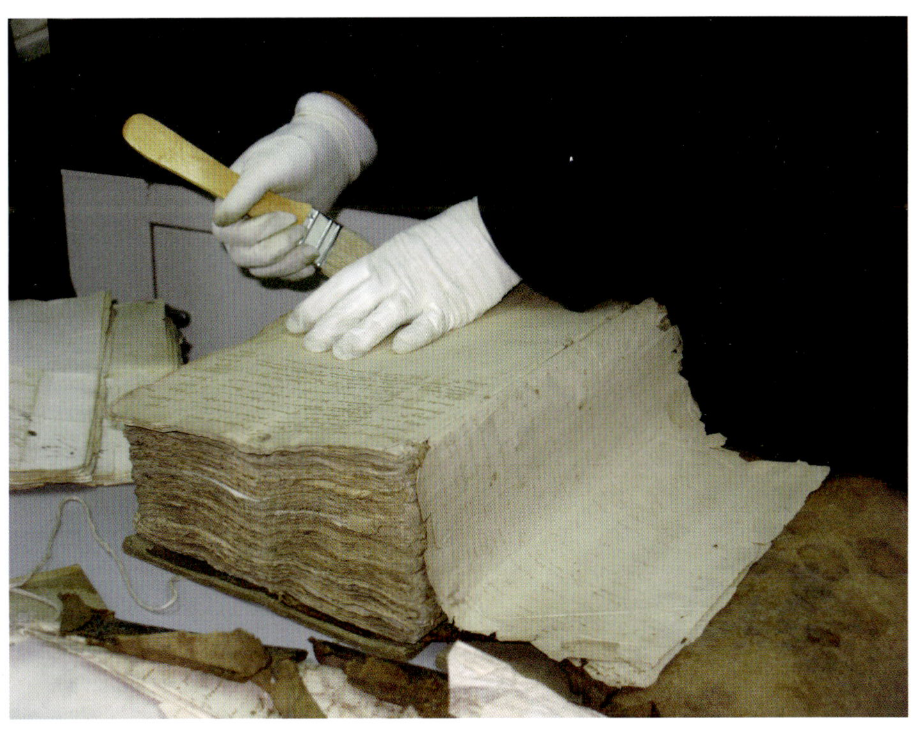

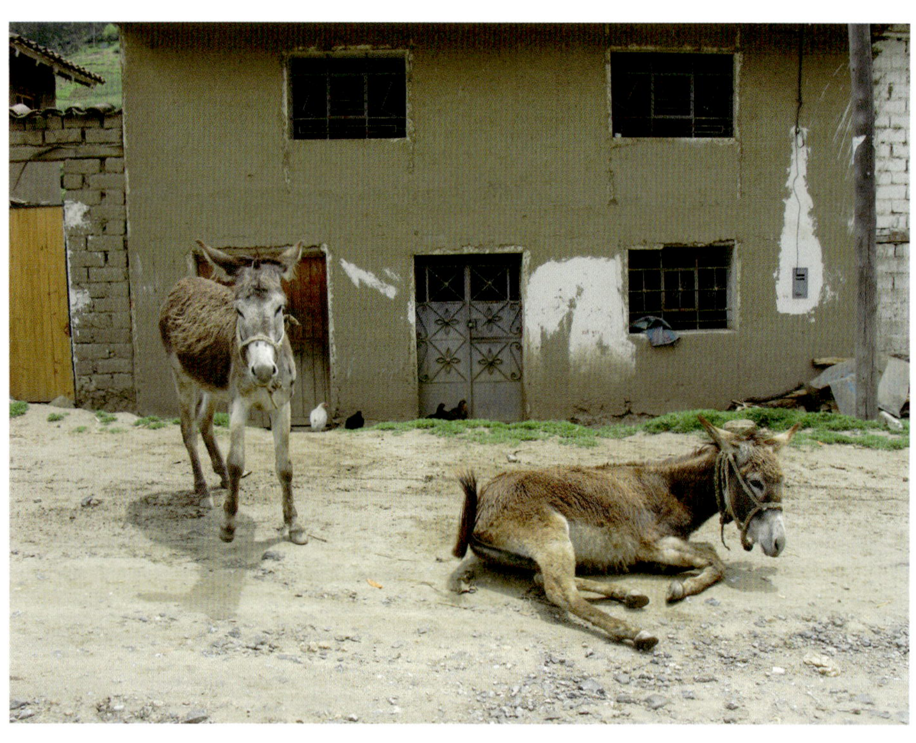

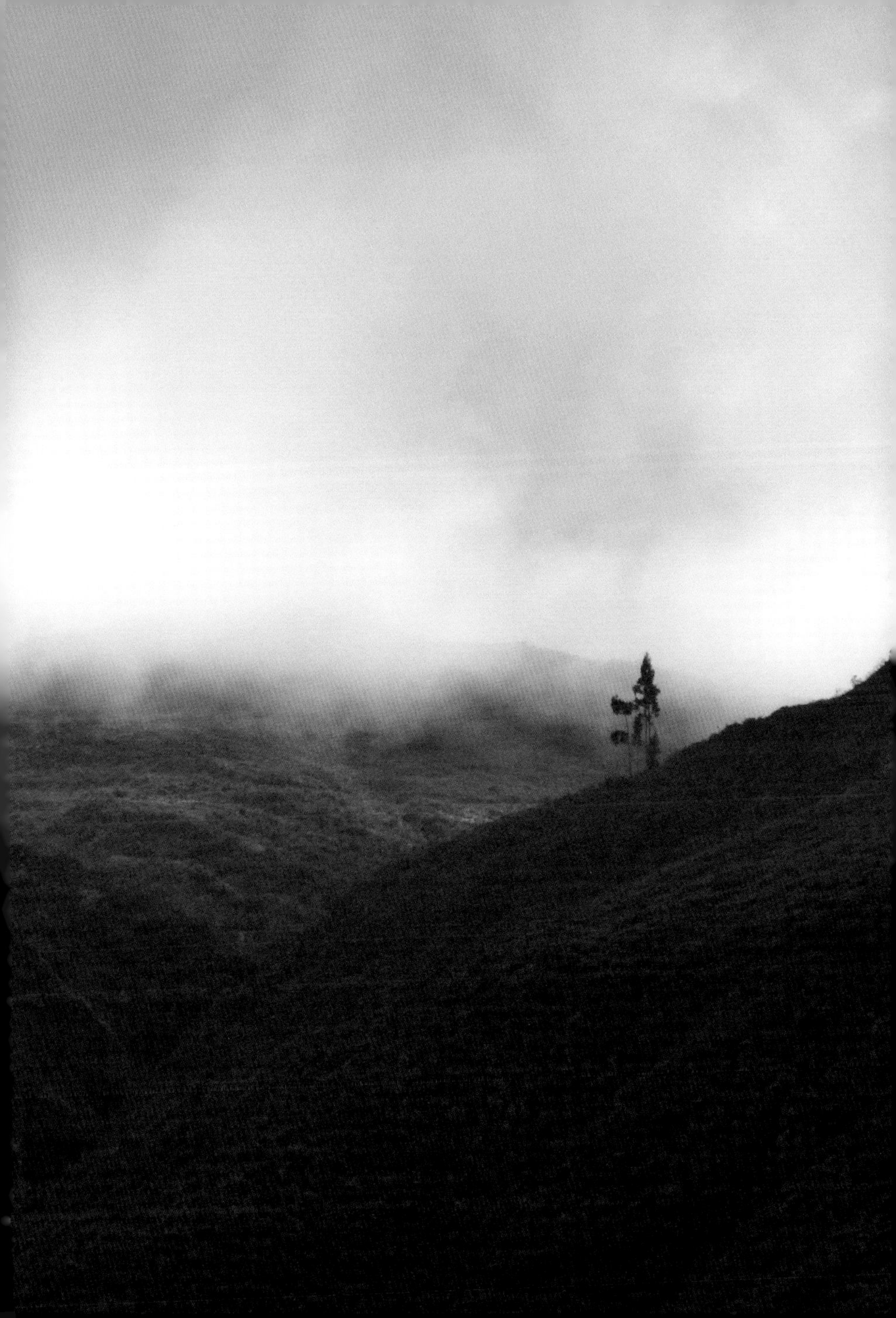

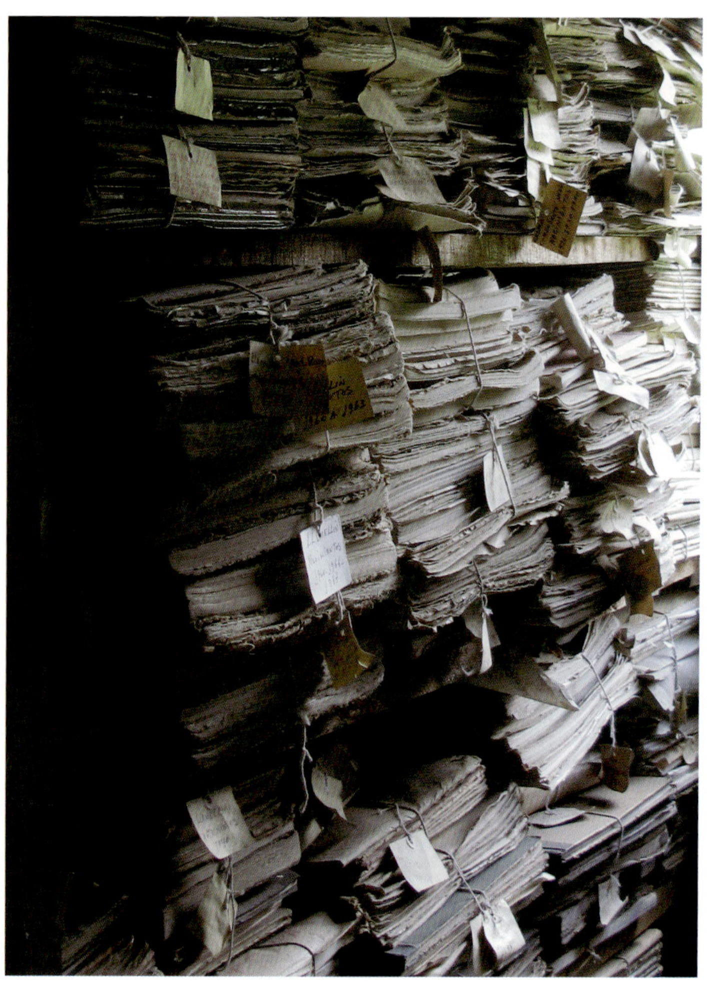

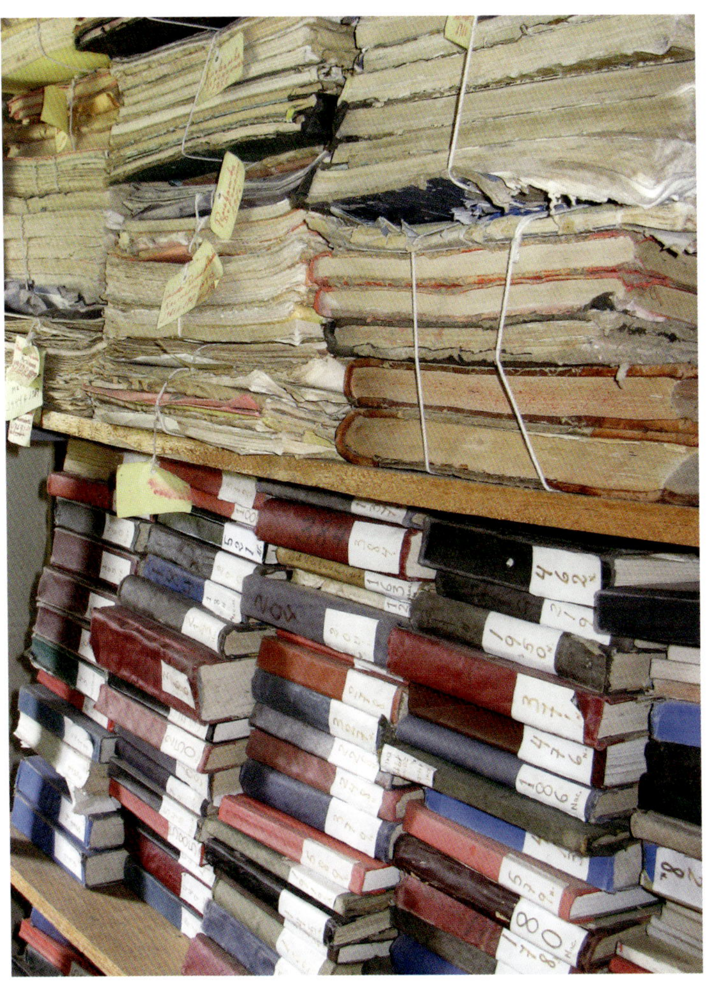

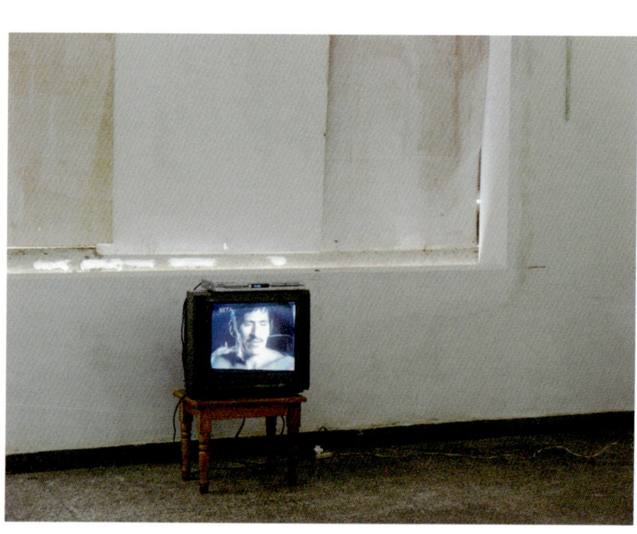

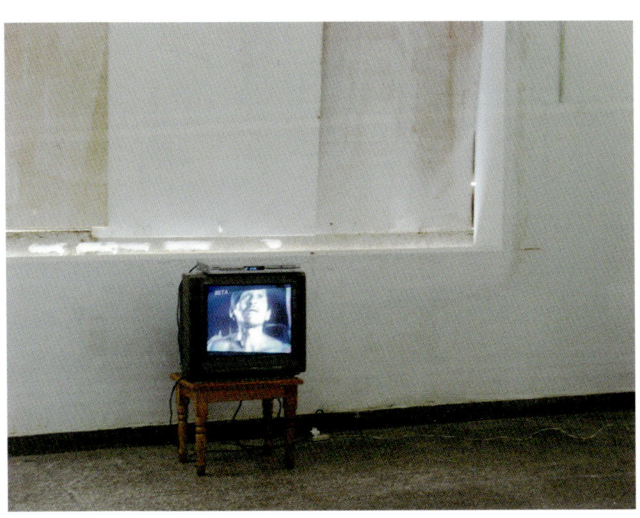

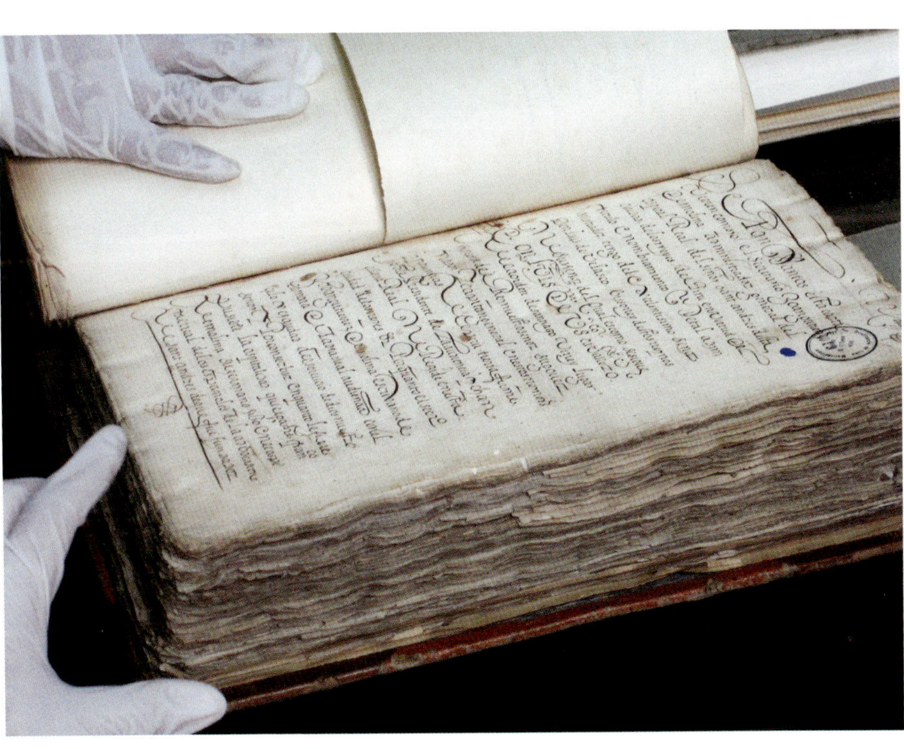

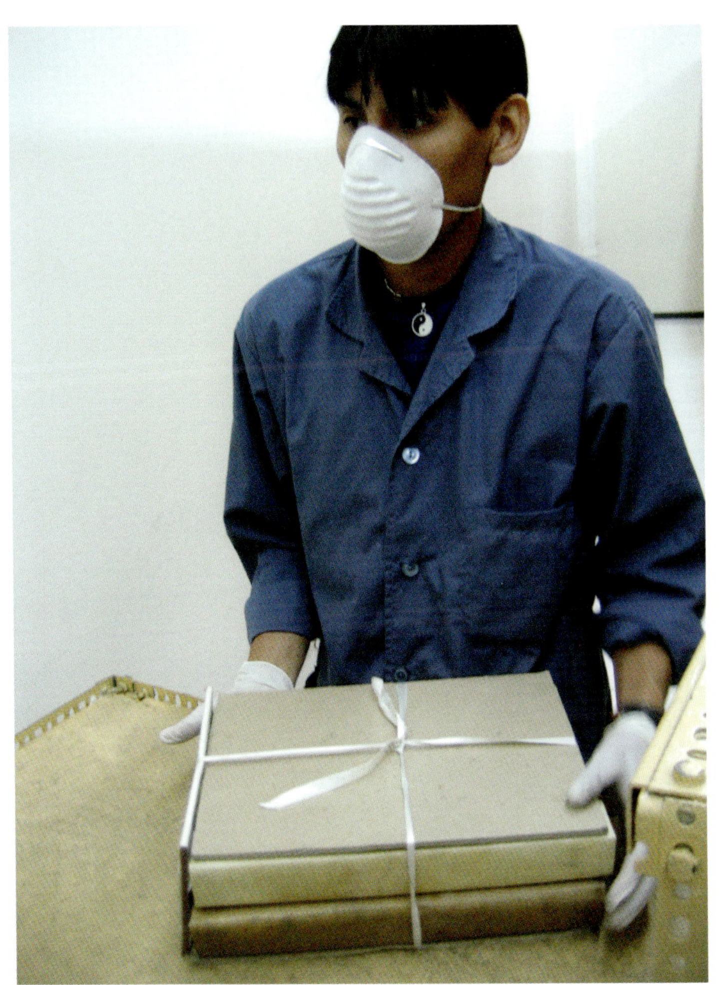

In 2008 I traveled to Peru with an anthropologist to work with an NGO based in Lima, and to meet with the National Archives to discuss their digitization program. Our goal was to assist in the preservation of important legal documents within their collections — specifically those related to indigenous land rights — and make them more widely accessible. Our second goal was to travel to a small village in the Andes to conduct workshops for the local population in preserving and digitizing their historical documents, as well as give guidance on how to gain access to the documents in the National Archives.

En route into the Andes, we took a detour and stopped at the ancient site of Caral to inspect the ruins from a mysteriously lost civilization, dating back roughly 5000 years. Fragmented petroglyphs were among the relics slowly being recovered.

Near the end of our stay, an agrarian workers' strike broke out. In protest to a long list of grievances, including a proposed law to privatize cultural patrimony, stones were littered across roadways to block passage.

ARCHIVE
Copyright © 2010 Danielle Mericle and A-Jump Books
Publisher: A-Jump Books, Ithaca, NY
Printed by: Oddi Printing, Reykjavik, Iceland
Edition of 500
First printing

Thank you Ron Jude, Shawn Records, and Patti Mericle for your ongoing support and invaluable input and assistance with this project. A special thanks to Billie Jean Isbell and Florencia Zapata for making this work possible, and for being such generous traveling companions. Lastly, thanks to all the people we met in Peru, for graciously hosting us and sharing with us your history, culture, and lives.

ISBN 978-0-9777655-5-3

A-JUMP BOOKS
www.a-jumpbooks.com • info@a-jumpbooks.com
www.dmericle.com